Successful
Project
Management
in a week

MARK BROWN

Hodder & Stoughton

A MEMBER OF THE HODDER HEADLINE GROUP

Acknowledgement

The author gratefully acknowledges Symantec (UK) Limited for permission to use TIMELINE to produce The Gantt Charts and Dependency Diagrams in this book.

The author would like to thank his wife, Mandi, who has suffered with great fortitude more projects than most marriages can bear.

Orders: please contact Bookpoint Ltd, 130 Milton Park, Abingdon, Oxon OX14 4SB. Telephone: (44) 01235 400414, Fax: (44) 01235 400454. Lines are open from 9.00 – 6.00, Monday to Saturday, with a 24 hour message answering service. Email address: orders@bookpoint.co.uk

British Library Cataloguing in Publication Data
Brown, Mark
Successful project management in a week
– (Business in a week)
I. Title   II. Series
658.4

ISBN 0 340 70539 6

First published 1992
Second edition 1998
Impression number   11   10   9   8   7
Year   2004   2003   2002   2001

© 1992, 1998 Mark Brown

Typeset by Multiplex Techniques Ltd, St Mary Cray, Kent.
Printed in Great Britain for Hodder & Stoughton Educational, a division of Hodder Headline Plc, 338 Euston Road, London NW1 3BH by Cox & Wyman Ltd, Reading, Berks.

໐
in *the Institute*
of Management

The Institute of Management (IM) is the leading
organisation for professional management.
Its purpose is to promote the art and science of
management in every sector and at every level,
through research, education, training and
development, and representation of members'
views on management issues.

This series is commissioned by IM Enterprises
Limited, a subsidiary of the Institute of Management,
providing commercial services.

Management House,
Cottingham Road,
Corby,
Northants NN17 1TT
Tel: 01536 204222;
Fax: 01536 201651
Website: http://www.inst-mgt.org.uk

Registered in England no 3834492
Registered office: 2 Savoy Court, Strand,
London WC2R 0EZ

C O N T E N T S

Project management has developed a reputation for being something of a black art – a skill which can only be practised by professionals who are well-versed in all sorts of odd-sounding disciplines and techniques.

There is no reason why this should be so. Project management is the application of good management practices in a structured manner. The skill lies in identifying when the circumstances in which these practices should be applied, and the best way to do so.

This book looks at the main areas of project management. By understanding these areas and applying some of the techniques we can improve our chances of managing projects to a successful completion

The main areas of project management

- Understanding the nature of a project
- The role of the project manager
- Setting up a project
- Planning a project
- Controlling a project
- Using automated tools
- The personal qualities of the Project Manager
- Finishing a project successfully

Today we will look at the nature of a project and what distinguishes it from other forms of activity.

> *The nature of the project*
>
> - Distinguishing characteristics
> - A typical project life cycle
> - The role of the Project Manager
> - The benefits of a systematic approach

Before we can look at Project Management in any detail, we should understand what a project is and why Project Management is different from *routine* management activities.

To be given responsibility for a project can seem a daunting prospect. All too often your brief will have been given on a half page memorandum, or is the resolution of a committee meeting. It is for you to turn this into something concrete, something which is readily identifiable and, more to the point, something which is under your control.

The nature of a project

The most obvious characteristic of a project is that it has to achieve some particular purpose, and this is normally indicated in the project's name: The Channel Tunnel Project, the Airbus Project, the Canary Wharf Project, etc. This distinguishes it from routine activities which are part of an organisation's normal business, such as running the payroll, editing a daily newspaper or producing another ten thousand tins of beans.

We will discuss aims and objectives of projects as a particular subject later this week but for the time being it is probably most useful to think of a project as *an instrument of change*.

When the project is successfully completed it will have an impact on people's lives, by changing their working patterns or by changing their environment. Managing change is clearly different (and at times much harder) than managing the status quo and it is for this reason that projects are established to effect such change in a controlled manner.

Projects can vary hugely both in their subject and in their size. A project can range from putting a man onto the moon, to selecting a new coffee machine for the office. Projects exist in all sorts of different types of business, such as information systems, construction, finance, marketing, industrial research and local government.

Moreover, no two projects are the same. A project to develop this year's model family saloon may look suspiciously like last year's, but its objectives will be different, the circumstances will have changed and it will involve different people.

The main characteristics of a project are that it:

Main characteristics of a project

- Is an instrument of change
- Has a clearly identifiable start and finish
- Has a specific aim
- Results in something being delivered
- Is unique
- Is the responsibility of a single person or body
- Involves cost, resources and time
- Uses a wide variety of resources and skills

All of these characteristics will not necessarily be obvious when a project is initiated. We may know the specific aim, but we will be aware of hidden agendas. Even if we have been given a budget and a deadline, we may still have little idea of the real cost, resource and time considerations of the project. All of these will have to be verified during the early part of the project.

Perhaps the only thing that the Project Manager can be sure of is that it is his responsibility and he will be judged by its success or failure.

A typical project life cycle

To help us apply some form of structure to the project, it is useful to think of all projects as having the same basic underlying structure. Whatever the project, it will pass through a number of distinct phases.

THE BUCK STOPS HERE

The nature of these phases will, of course, vary depending on the type of project. So too will the time taken to go through them, from minutes to years.

Typically, a project will begin as the result of a report or feasibility study. (The work to undertake the feasibility study may well itself have been run as an individual project.)

The feasibility study will have defined the problem which is being addressed (such as 'It takes too long to cross the Channel', or 'we cannot reconcile our month-end figures until six weeks after month-end'). It may have investigated what the real requirements are (e.g. 'We need to be able to cross the Channel in less than one hour'). It will have evaluated alternative solutions and recommended a course of action.

The remaining phases of the project are as follows:

Typical project phases

- Initiation
- Specification
- Design
- Build
- Installation/implementation
- Operation and review

Initiation

Initiation is the most important phase of any project. Unless it is carried out effectively, the project stands little chance of success.

Initiation covers such areas as defining the terms of reference, setting objectives, agreeing budgets and gaining project approval. We will discuss this in more detail tomorrow, but it is enough to say here that the initiation of a project represents its very foundation. The manner in which it is conducted will set the tone for the remainder of the project.

It can also be the most intense period for the Project Manager, and much of this book is devoted to the activities inherent in it.

Specification

Specification is the phase of a project where the detailed requirements are determined. It is a time when you will be in close contact with the ultimate users of the project deliverable.

The project team will be analysing the users' requirements in detail and these will be documented by a Requirements Specification, which will be signed-off by the user. This will form the definitive scope of the remainder of the project.

It is at this point that the user tells you in precise terms what he wants you to deliver. It is important to note, however, that at this stage we are only concerned with the 'what' and not with the 'how'. Here he will say that he needs to be able to get a container from London to Paris in four hours; it is not until the Design phase that you start talking about tunnels and bridges, lorries and trains.

Because you have a clearer idea of what the project involves, you will also have a better idea of what the costs and time considerations are likely to be. Typically, you will return to the project sponsor – with more detailed information and more detailed plans – to seek approval to proceed further.

Design
It is at the *design* phase that the 'what' is translated into the 'how'. Gradually, the final deliverable is beginning to take shape. Armed with the agreed requirements, the technical experts – architects, systems analysts, engineers, physicists – will create a solution for the problem which had been expressed.

This design forms the blueprint for the next phase. It may come in a variety of forms; diagrammatic plans, a working model, a prototype, or a detailed specification.

As in the previous phase, the design is agreed with the user and more detailed plans are developed for the next phase.

Build

Finally something tangible is created: the tunnel is dug, the building erected, or the system built. The *build* phase is the period which is awaited with the most impatience. There will always be a temptation to skimp on initiation, specification and design, merely to be seen to be producing something. *This is a temptation to be resisted.*

Implementation

The product has been designed and built and is now almost ready to be put into operation. Although we will have continually verified that what we're building is what the user actually asked for, a final acceptance process will take place during this phase.

Here we will also apply any transition procedures which need to be effected. Remember, project management is about the management of change. It is all very well developing lead-free petrol, but cars have to be modified, customers educated and prices set.

Operation

The operation phase is often overlooked as not being part of the project itself. It should not, however, be neglected. Once we are satisfied that the product works, that the ship didn't sink when the bottle of champagne struck its bow, then the project is over. As in the case of all the previous phases something is delivered: a final report which details the findings of a post implementation review.

Once your new product has been in use for a while – and probably not a very long while at that – new problems and requirements will emerge, and the whole cycle will begin again.

The role of the Project Manager

The role of a manager, any manager, is well understood to be as follows:

The role of the manager:

- To plan
- To organise
- To co-ordinate
- To control
- To lead

All this is equally applicable to a Project Manager. The distinction, however, is that he is fulfilling these roles in order to bring about change and not to preserve the status quo.

Planning, organisation, co-ordination and control outside of a project environment such as managing a department which operates in a functional role (e.g. sales, production or accounts) are frequently constrained by the process itself, by the activities of other departments, or by conflicting demands within the department.

Although no less true for project management, there is a shift of emphasis in which the above roles are all tightly focused on achieving the project's aim, and that the project is closely allied with the business objectives of the organisation.

A large part of this effort will manifest itself in the role of *communicator*.

Gaining and maintaining sponsorship
Having an influential sponsor for the project is critical to its success. This applies particularly to longer projects.

Your project is likely to be competing for management attention with a number of other projects and activities within the organisation. An influential senior manager who will champion both you and your project will ensure that you receive appropriate senior management support. In this way, when you need decisions to be made, approvals to be granted, or resources to be made available, your project will not always be bottom of the agenda.

Particularly in dynamic and rapidly changing organisations, it is easy for the world to move faster than your project. Whilst your project may have been flavour of the month when it was initiated, it may no longer be so a year later – even if the need for it genuinely remains the same – as newer and more exciting projects appear.

Advertising the project

This is very closely related to gaining sponsorship, but applies to all levels of the organisation. The Project Manager has a responsibility to ensure that the credibility of his project is maintained at all times, and that the project maintains a high profile within the organisation throughout its lifetime.

The Project Manager is likely to be the main link between the project team and the outside world, and it is important that he makes a point of promoting the project.

Managing user expectations

It is inevitable on large projects – particularly long ones – that the users' perceptions of what you are going to deliver will differ from your own understanding. Regular reviews and control checkpoints (particularly at the end of each phase) will go a long way to avoiding this.

User expectations can vary enormously from complete cynicism to wild over-optimism about the way in which their lives will be enhanced when the project delivers.

It is vital to the success of the project that these excesses are curtailed. Users should be involved in all aspects of the project so that a relationship can be built that allows effective two-way communication.

Remember, in the end it is the users' reaction to what you deliver that is the prime determinant of whether your project was a success or failure.

A systematic approach

Having described projects as being fundamentally unique, varying in size, shape, time, cost and resources, it may seem odd that we should attempt to describe a standard project management approach which is universally applicable. But it is because of this variety that a systematic approach is necessary.

Benefits of a systematic approach

- It ensures that the product which the project is to deliver is clearly defined and understood by all parties
- It enables the objectives of the project to be clearly defined and closely allied to the business objectives of the organisation
- It allows responsibilities for different parts of the project to be understood, allocated and agreed
- It promotes a logical approach to planning and encourages more accurate estimating
- It provides a consistent means by which monitoring and control can be effected
- It reassures senior management by demonstrating visible control

Project initiation

Today we will look at the beginning of a project. As we discussed yesterday, the initiation phase of the project is the most important phase. Get this wrong and the project will almost certainly fail.

Project initiation

- Setting objectives
- Defining the scope
- Establishing the strategy
- Deriving the work breakdown structure

The key to Project Initiation is the Terms of Reference document. This may manifest itself in a number of guises – such as the recommendations of a feasibility study or project definition report – but it is important that it is given proper attention.

In many ways, the Terms of Reference represents the Project Manager's contract with the users and with the project's sponsor. As such it serves to define the context of the project, what is expected and when.

The Terms of Reference is the first point at which a form of structure is applied to the project; it is given shape, size and direction, even if only in general terms.

Terms of reference

... IN THE BEGINNING, NOBODY HAD SET ANY OBJECTIVES, LET ALONE DONE THE COSTING, AND THERE WAS DARKNESS...

Key elements of the Terms of Reference

- Authority and project sponsor
- Customer
- Objectives
- Scope
- Constraints
- Costs/budget
- Resources
- Deliverables
- Project phases and timescales
- Strategy
- Risks
- Roles and responsibilities

Authority and project sponsor

This needs to be no more than a simple statement describing who has asked that the project be carried out. Depending on the position of the project in the organisation – which we will discuss later – there may be times during the life of the project where you have to seek a decision from a higher authority, for example, to resolve conflicting priorities. It is as well to have this higher authority, and the authority which is delegated to the Project Manager, defined at the outset.

Customer

Over and above the Project Sponsor, it is important to be quite clear as to who you are doing this project for; who is the project's *customer*. This will usually be the final user of the product which you are delivering.

Objectives

Reasons for setting objectives

- To provide direction
- To focus on results
- To enable plans to be made
- To prioritise and organise work
- To motivate staff
- To communicate the purpose of the project
- To enable success to be recognised

We discussed on Sunday the role of the Project Manager in gaining and retaining sponsorship for the project. A key aspect of retaining the support of the organisation is to ensure that the objectives of the project coincide with the business objectives of the organisation. This alignment of objectives should be explicit, and describe precisely how the project will contribute to the business.

Objectives come in a variety of shapes and sizes: they can be strategic or tactical, technical or procedural, open or secret, long-term or short-term, applicable to the organisation or very personal, so it is difficult to generalise about them. However, here are some basic rules for the definition of project objectives:

Project objectives should

- Be aligned to business objectives
- Be measurable, in terms of
  - quality
  - quantity
  - time
  - cost
  - defined end product
- Be achievable
- Be consistent
- Be readily understandable
- Be few in number
- Have the full support and commitment of senior management, project sponsor and users

Project objectives should never suffer from vagueness or over-generalisation. If we are to know whether or not a project has been successful we must know whether our objectives have been achieved.

Measurable objectives
These measures of success are sometimes considered so important that you may find them as a separate section in the Terms of Reference. A project to develop a more fuel-efficient engine should state clearly *how much* more efficient that engine should be. A project to improve productivity should state *how many* extra widgets will be produced an hour, or what the cost savings will be.

Achievable objectives

It is clearly in the Project Manager's interests that the objectives are achievable and he should satisfy himself that this is so. If the objectives are not, then it suggests that the wrong project, perhaps in terms of scale or scope, has been selected.

Consistent objectives

It is not so obvious that we should think to ensure that our objectives are consistent. Business objectives often contain inherent inconsistencies – increasing shareholder return is not always consistent with a substantial R & D investment (at least in the short term) – and it is possible that your project objectives may suffer from similar inherent contradictions.

Where objectives appear inconsistent you should state what the priorities are, and what trade-offs are acceptable. All Project Managers must take a view on the relationships between their objectives relating to Time, Cost and Quality.

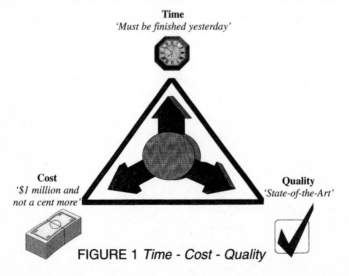

Time
'Must be finished yesterday'

Cost
'$1 million and not a cent more'

Quality
'State-of-the-Art'

FIGURE 1 *Time - Cost - Quality*

This is the 'eternal triangle' of project management, and the Project Manager will constantly be engaged in some form of trade-off between these objectives. Where you position yourself within the triangle depends on the project: if you are producing commemorative plates for the Millenium you are likely to be near the top of the triangle, if you are developing safety-critical systems you may find yourself in the bottom right of the triangle.

Although it is useful to be able to say to yourself 'I am more concerned about time than cost', you should try to quantify this, if it has not already been imposed upon you; e.g. 'I have a budget of between £1,000,000 and £1,500,000, but come what may I have to deliver a working product in time for the Christmas sales drive.'

Scope

Unless clearly defined at the outset, an ill-defined scope is one of the areas likely to cause most trouble during the course of the project.

Scope can be defined in a number of ways and rarely can a single line be drawn to say what is inside and what is outside of the project. On Sunday, we discussed how project management is the management of change, so we must define our scope in terms of the things which we are going to change:

Scope can be defined in terms of:

- Departments affected
- People affected
- Locations or regions affected
- Business processes affected
- Products affected

This can be thought of as the 'Who, Where, When and What' of the project. A well-defined scope will stop you trying to solve the wrong problems, or wasting time on work which is not relevant.

A project to automate administration within a health authority may in the first instance cover only: 1) medical records departments; 2) hospitals in the south of the area; 3) admissions and appointments procedures; and 4) out-patients.

During the course of the project there will usually be pressures to change the scope. For this reason, your original scope should be clearly defined at the outset, and in this way you can more easily assess the impact of any change in the scope.

Constraints

Constraints are very similar to scope, but express what areas are outside of the scope, or what boundaries you may not cross. Time and cost limitations are common, and these invariably have an impact on the third factor, quality.

Constraints may also be the result of external forces over which you have no control: the law, geography, organisational etiquette, etc.

Costs

At this stage you may have little idea as to what the costs of the project will be. There may well, however, be a budget for the project, and this should be reflected in the Terms of Reference.

Resources

Again, you will not know precisely what resources will be required. You should, however, state from where you intend to staff the project – internally or externally, for which departments – and any particular resource or skill needs which are already apparent.

Deliverables

STAND AND DELIVER!

Project deliverables should be explicitly defined so that there is no doubt in the minds of senior management, users or the project staff what is expected. It is not enough, for example, to say that you will deliver a computer system: you will be delivering software, hardware, manuals, and training.

Additionally, there will usually be interim deliverables during the course of the project; documentation, research results, prototypes, designs and models.

Interim deliverables have the benefit of being tangible evidence of progress during the course of the project. As such, their production normally coincides with the end of a significant project phase or milestone.

Project phases and timescales

You should at this point be able to identify the main phases of the project, even if it is only at the level at which we described it on Sunday. You may choose to change the names of the phases, to make them more appropriate to your project or to your organisation's culture. But now, having given more thought to what the project is about, you should now be in a position to set some approximate timescales.

Phasing a project allows the work to be seen in more understandable components. Particularly in the case of long projects, it is easy for both project staff and senior management to lose their sense of commitment if the project end date is a very long way off.

It is, of course, difficult to say at this stage exactly how long any phase will take. The further down the road into the project the less information you have now, and the less reliable any estimate can be. Typically you will confine yourself to committing to a date for your first phase, and providing indicative dates for subsequent ones.

Strategy

Having defined your objectives, scope, deliverables, phases and timescales, your project is already beginning to take shape. However, you have yet to define how it is that you intend to pursue the project.

It is important that this is agreed in advance. Although you may be given a fairly free rein, senior management will need to have a degree of confidence in the approach that you are taking. Likewise, your own project staff (and other staff whose cooperation they will depend on) will require some high level guiding principles for the project.

Your strategy should include:

Strategic principles:

- The use of any particular techniques or methodologies
- The adoption of any recognised standards
- Relationships with other parts of the organisation

Risks

The identification of *risks* in a Terms of Reference or Project Definition Statement is not intended as an opportunity for the Project Manager to say 'I told you so !' if his project fails.

It is, however an opportunity to consider what may be major problems in the project, and what can be done at this stage to ameliorate their impact or likelihood.

It may be that you are trying to do something particularly innovative, that you are adopting a new methodology, that you are subject to something totally out of your control (such as a stock market crash on the day you launch a rights issue, or the unexpected introduction of new legislation).

Risk analysis is a major subject in its own right. However, for the purposes of project initiation it should suffice to be able to do the following:

Risk analysis

- Identify the risks
- Assess the chances of each occurring
- Assess the impact on the project/organisation if the risks do occur
- Identify measures which can be taken to prevent them occurring
- Identify contingency arrangements which can ameliorate their effects if the risks do occur

---

Assumptions
Any assumptions which are made at this stage should be clearly expressed as these are, in themselves, elements of risk.

Dependencies
You should include in your risk analysis any dependencies on external factors over which you have no or limited

control. This may be a dependency on another part of your organisation to provide a resource at a particular time, or a dependency on an external supplier to provide a product or part required for your project.

These dependencies will be detailed in the roles and responsibilities section of the Terms of Reference, but referring to them as risks can help to ensure that your project sponsor and senior management are aware of the impact of failing to ensure that other parts of the organisation are committed to your project.

Contingency
Contingency arrangements to allow for risks can be as simple as adding 10 per cent onto the expected project duration to allow for anything going wrong, or may be elaborate fall-back plans, or descoping of the project.

If contingency time is added onto plans – and it is not always appropriate to do so – great care must be taken as to who is aware of this. Clearly, it must be agreed with the project sponsor, but you must guard against the onset of Parkinson's Law (work filling available time) if it becomes common knowledge that 'no-one is really going to mind if the project is a month late'.

Roles and responsibilities

External resources
At this stage, you will have given little detailed thought to how the project will be staffed and organised – this comes later. It is important, though, to ensure that all external roles and responsibilities are made clear.

No project can exist in isolation and you will always require the cooperation of others, either within the organisation or from outside. Other people's involvement in your project can be to: execute specific pieces of work, provide information, take decisions or be available for consultation.

You should indicate when and how much involvement is required so that other people can plan to make the appropriate resources available when you need them. If you fail to do this you run the considerable risk of having those resources denied when you need them most.

Decision-making responsibilities
Establishing who decides what is a major prerequisite for any project. If clear decision-making responsibilities are not defined then either crucial decisions will not be made and the project will suffer from inertia, or the project team itself will take decisions, resulting in alienation and reduced commitment from the users.

As a general rule, decisions should be made by those who normally make them within the organisation, or have some accountability for the consequences. Accountants should make decisions about the accounts, technicians about technical problems, etc.

Levels of authority should also be defined, especially authority to spend money or deviate from the Terms of Reference. This should include escalation procedures to help resolve conflicts between irreconcilable decisions made by different decision-makers.

Project organisation

Having established what the project is and what it is setting
out to do, we now have to consider *how* we are going to
achieve it. Much of the work described in the previous two
days has been concerned with establishing the appropriate
environment for the project. Today we will look inward into
the project itself and discuss organising the project and the
first stage of the planning process. This is covered by the
following topics:

Project organisation and high level planning

- Work breakdown structure
- Project organisation
- Outline plan and milestones

Work breakdown structure

The Work Breakdown Structure (WBS) is a key document in
the project and forms the basis of much of the subsequent
work in planning, setting budgets, financial control,
defining the organisation and assigning responsibilities.

Its development relies on the gradual decomposition of the
project into units of work. We will already have mapped out
the high level phases which the project will go through, and
these represent the first level of breakdown.

Breaking the project down into manageable units is the key
to being able to control it. Projects suffer from the 'Salami
Syndrome'; i.e. when they are viewed as a whole they are

rather unattractive, but when cut into fine slices they become quite appetising.

Through the process of gradually dividing a piece of work up into something more manageable we will finally arrive at discrete pieces of work which we will be able to estimate, plan and control.

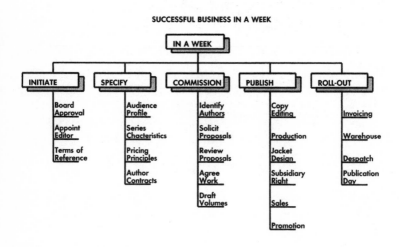

FIGURE 2 *Work Breakdown Structure*

Levels

Each different level of the WBS is often given a name such as phase, activity, or task. These names will vary between organisations, but it is important to be consistent when referring to them.

How many levels you arrive at will vary from project to project; generally the bigger the project the more levels you have. It is, therefore, difficult to be prescriptive: up to about five is fine, more than that and perhaps you should be thinking of initiating sub-projects to deal with different legs of the WBS. Anything over ten levels and the project scope is probably flawed.

Completeness
At this point the Project Manager will have to involve other people, who will probably end up as part of the project team. Except in the case of trivial projects, it is inconceivable that the Project Manager will be able to derive the WBS on his own as he will not have the necessary detailed knowledge of each area. Although we may consider ourselves to be experts in particular fields, generally no one individual should work on more than two levels.

T U E S D A Y

One of the main objectives of the WBS is to identify all the pieces of work which need to be undertaken to complete the project. It is important, therefore, that identification of the work to be done is carried out by those people who are most familiar with the processes involved. So the Project Manager might define the first two levels, heads of departments or team leaders the next, a senior engineer the next, and so on.

Occasionally you may be able to 'borrow' a WBS from a previous (similar) project. This will help, but should only be used as a final check-list to ensure that you haven't forgotten anything. Remember, *projects are unique*.

Projects fail more often because activities were not planned at the outset, than because activities were planned badly. Naturally, there will be changes during the course of the project, but there should not be any purely as a result of forgetting that something needed to be done.

Work unit characteristics
The nature of the work units will obviously differ as one works down the hierarchy; at the higher levels will appear phases which are probably discrete. These will result in major deliverables and constitute significant review points throughout the project.

At the lower levels they will be shorter in duration and be less 'self-standing'. What is produced by them will probably be an integral part of something else.

A great asset of this hierarchical levelling is that the WBS can be used as a communication tool at different levels in the hierarchy. The Managing Director may not be terribly interested in knowing when the wheels of the car are built, but he will certainly be interested in knowing when the overall design phase is finished.

We can, however, say that if we are to arrive at sensible tasks (particularly at the bottom level of the WBS) the tasks should conform to the following criteria. They should:

Task characteristics

- Be measurable in terms of cost, effort, resource and time
- Result in a single (verifiable) end product
- Have clear start and end dates
- Be the responsibility of a single person

The existence of the end product is sometimes a difficult thing to insist upon as this will not always be something tangible and, as a Project Manager, you will need to be able to satisfy yourself that a particular task has been completed.

On-going tasks such as management or administration should be included in the WBS as these will have an effect on the project budget, even if they will not affect the project schedule.

You should also include tasks which are being undertaken outside of the immediate project area, such as reviewing of documentation by outsiders.

Whilst at this stage we are only interested in the existence of the tasks, we should also be collecting as much information about them as we can. This should include:

Task information

- Description of task
- Necessary inputs or preconditions
- Deliverables
- Particular resource requirements (with costs)
- Particular skill requirements
- Responsibilities
- Estimated time

It is often convenient to have this information recorded on a standardised form (see Figure 3) which can be maintained on the Project File.

Project organisation

Having established the WBS you will now have a fairly detailed view of what the project looks like; in particular, what needs to be done.

The next stage is determining who is going to do it and how they should be organised. Although it would be wrong to suggest that correct organisation will solve all your problems it is without doubt that a flawed organisation will cause major problems on a project.

These will manifest themselves as difficulties in communication, responsibility or commitment. The organisation you select for your projects should, therefore, try to address these issues.

TASK DEFINITION

WBS Code	TASK NAME

DELIVERABLE	
Description	Quality Standard
Customer	Needed by date

DEPENDENCIES		
Event/Deliverable	Dependency Type	Deliverer

START DATE		END DATE	

RESOURCING		
Days Effort	Skills / Job Title	Optimum Staffing

COSTS		RESPONSIBILITIES	
Staff		Project Management	
External Suppliers		Delivery	
Professional Fees		Quality	
Fixed			
TOTAL			

ADDITIONAL INFORMATION / COMMENT

Author		Department	
Location		Tel.	

FIGURE 3 *Task Definition Form*

Logically, your WBS is your project organisation. We stated that for each work unit which appeared on the WBS there was a single person responsible for the delivery of the end product associated with it. We should, therefore, be able to map bottom level tasks onto individual workers, higher-level tasks onto their managers, and so on.

Function-based Organisation

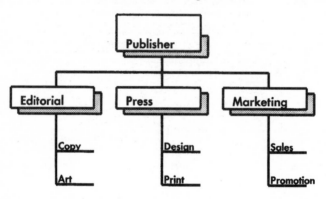

Work Breakdown Structure

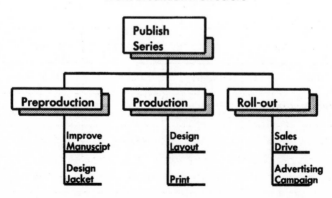

FIGURE 4 *Hierarchical Organisation Structure*

At first sight this implies a *hierarchical* project structure, and this is indeed a common means of organising projects. But it can also be applied to a *matrix* organisation.

Matrix project organisation

PROJECTS / DEPARTMENTS	PROJECT ALPHA	PROJECT BETA	PROJECT GAMMA
REQUIREMENTS	Jones	Jones	Brown
DESIGN	Williams	Smith	Smith
PROGRAMMING	Shannon	Black	Black
TESTING	O'Dee	O'Dee	O'Dee
IMPLEMENTATION	Thomas	Price	Philips

FIGURE 5 *Matrix Organisational Structure*

The matrix approach leaves staff working on the project within their own departmental structures. It allows the project to remain fully integrated with the mainstream organisation, and encourages decision-making to remain within the organisation, rather than isolated within the project.

In order to avoid a conflict of priorities and accountabilities there needs to be clear agreement between the project management and the departmental management about the amount of time and commitment that individual members of staff can spend on the project.

Whilst the hierarchical structure may on the face of it appear to be an easier one for the Project Manager to control, as all the resources are under his or her direct management, the matrix approach goes a long way to ameliorating those 'soft' problems which often beset projects.

The Project Office
The role of a Project Office is to co-ordinate the activities which are being undertaken in functional departments for the project. It will therefore control:

Project Office co-ordination functions

- Preparation of plans
- Reporting of progress against plans and budgets
- Resolution of dependencies and issues
- Management of changes and enhancements
- Preparation of standards and quality control
- Tracking and resolution of issues

This is more than a simple administrative role, and should be fulfilled by a staff who see themselves as extensions of the Project Manager; acting as his eyes and ears and intervening where appropriate.

A certain amount of administration is, however, unavoidable. To avoid descending into a bureaucracy which stifles productivity, administration should be kept as simple as possible. It is useful to bring into the Project Office all those tasks which can be usefully centralised. This might include time sheet keeping, document control, project library, organising and minuting meetings and maintaining the project diary.

You should, however, make the Project Office's accountabilities clear; they can be responsible for facilitating the resolution of issues, but cannot be held accountable if issues remain unresolved.

The milestone plan

Having defined the structure of the project and the WBS, it is important to begin to focus the project on results.

Particularly in the case of lengthy projects, the final delivery of the end product will seem a long way off and it is, therefore, difficult to instil a sense of urgency amongst people working on the project. You should therefore define intermediate targets, or *milestones*, towards the overall aim.

Defining milestones will assist the Project Manager in a number of ways:

The purpose of milestones

- To provide a measure of progress on the project which is accessible to senior management
- To provide a means of communication with people outside the project team
- To focus project attention on results
- To provide manageable stages of work
- To enable responsibilities to be apportioned at a high level

The actual definition of milestones and the relationships between them – the dependencies – should be done by members of the project team working together. A 'brainstorming' session might be appropriate as this will encourage commitment to the plan by those involved.

By starting at the end of the project – the final deliverable – and working backwards, you should identify the major points through which you must pass.

Milestones represent particular points in the project, and as such should be expressed in the form *'When X has happened'*. This may be the production of the end product at the end of a phase, a major decision having been taken, or a document having been accepted.

Because they are a part of the project which the Project Manager will be controlling directly, and probably the most visible at that, milestones should be readily verifiable and there should be no doubt about whether or not the milestone has been reached.

It is easy to think that a document has been finished when the last word has been written, but in practice work will continue on it while it is reviewed, revised and agreed. Your milestones should recognise this.

The milestones do not represent a detailed plan of the project. Their number will depend on the size of the project but between 10 and 20 – corresponding to the second level of the WBS – will probably be enough to demonstrate the whole project adequately. These should be spaced at controllable intervals of between a fortnight and a month, again depending on the nature and size of the project.

Detailed planning

Today we will look at the more detailed aspects of planning
and the tools which are available to help you with this.

Detailed planning stages

- Estimating
- Identifying dependencies
- Constructing the dependency network
- Assigning responsibilities
- Allocating resources
- Producing a Gantt Chart
- Refining the plan

Planning requires a large amount of information, and the
amount and quality of information which you will have is
inversely proportional to the length of time between when
you plan and when the tasks should be executed.

For anything but the very smallest of projects you will
normally only provide a detailed plan for the project phase
that you are about to enter. Typically, planning the next
phase will be one of the last tasks of all phases of the project.

Estimating

Effective estimating is the key to a plan in which one can
have a degree of confidence. It is also one of the hardest
parts as it involves making judgements based on
knowledge, understanding and experience. As such,
different – and sometimes conflicting – interests come to the
fore.

Estimates will always be subject to human interpretation of these factors, and the Project Manager should ask himself the following questions:

If estimates appear too long

- Is the estimator trying to give himself more time than he really needs to make his own life easier?
- Is he unnessarily concerned (e.g. through lack of experience) about the complexity of the task?
- Is he planning to deliver what you would consider to be an over-engineered solution (e.g. a 200-page report when a one-page memorandum would suffice)?

If the estimates appear too short

- Is the estimator over-confident?
- Does he really appreciate the complexity?
- Does he fully appreciate what must be delivered?
- Has he made unreasonable assumptions?

To take account of the 'soft' human factors mentioned above, we should try to apply a degree of objectivity and empiricism to the process. No method of predicting the future is fail-safe, but by ensuring that we are taking *informed* judgements on the basis of sound data and reasonable assumptions we can reduce the risk.

There are many different techniques which can be used for estimating, each more or less appropriate to different circumstances. However, you should note that these can never be a substitute for judgement and experience.

If you do adopt a formalised estimating process – and it is usually appropriate that you do so – you should stick to it. Guard against the tendency of managers to inflate figures provided by their subordinates (if this is done at several levels in the hierarchy the figures can become widely unrepresentative of the true picture). Conversely, resist the temptation to impose arbitrary cuts; the pressure upon you to do this may be particularly great when working on a time-critical project.

Some of the main principles to be observed when estimating are described opposite:

Principles of estimating

- Estimates should be in terms of days effort (or 'man days'). The elapsed time taken to complete a task is a product of the resources which can be applied to it and other constraints
- Estimates should not include any allowance for contingency; that can be applied later at a global level
- Estimates should be 'honest'
- Individual commitment should be sought
- The skill and experience levels of the available staff should be allowed for
- The procedure used and any assumptions made should be documented
- The process should be revisited throughout the project to ensure that assumptions and factors used in the derivation of estimates still hold true
- Estimates should not be 'massaged'
- Always apply a reasonableness check

Estimating using historical data

Historical data about previous projects can be an invaluable source of base data for new projects. Generally, this data will only be available if your organisation has well-established planning and control procedures, which have faithfully recorded the time and effort spent on each task during previous projects.

Estimating using relative time

There is frequently a direct relationship between the time taken to do one task and the time taken to do a subsequent one. If it takes two months to design a particular type of product, then it might generally take four months to build it and a further two to test it.

Rules which specify these relationships may be well-known within your own industry.

Estimating using parameters
It is possible to derive formulae which can take into account the size of the deliverable and the complexity of the task. Some of these formulae are well-established in particular industries. In Information Technology there are well-known formulae based on the number of files a program will access, the number of decisions to be made within the program, and the language being used.

These formulae are often derived and refined using many years of historical data.

Dependencies

On any project some tasks will be performable concurrently and some must be done in a clear order. Defining dependencies is the process by which we identify the order in which things must be done.

Typically the way to do this is to start at the end of the project and work backwards, saying at each task 'What must be in place before I can begin this task'. Gradually you will establish predecessors for every task until you arrive at the beginning.

This is not necessarily a straightforward exercise, as you will find tasks dependent on multiple predecessors, half-done predecessors and other complications.

There are four basic types of dependency relationship:

Types of dependency relationship

- Finish to start – in which the preceding task must be completed before the succeeding one can start
- Start to finish – in which the preceding task must start before the succeeding one can finish
- Finish to finish – in which both tasks must finish simultaneously
- Start to start – in which both tasks must start simultaneously

Because relationships are not always as clear cut as this, you should also be able to identify cases where there is a particular amount of overlap. Thus we might say that Task B might start one week into Task A.

All good planning tools will allow you to record this information.

FROM THE (Start/End) OF THE PREDECESSOR: Dig Foundations
(Add/Subtract) [0] (Minutes/Hours/Days/Weeks/Months)
THEN (Start/End) THE SUCCESSOR: Build Walls

Dependency networks

By establishing dependencies between predecessors and successors we can establish dependency networks. These are also known as PERT (Program Evaluation and Review Technique) charts.

Uses of dependency networks

- To determine the critical path
- To determine the shortest time in which the project could be delivered
- To identify tasks which represent particular risks
- To identify periods when too much may be happening
- To enhance your understanding of the project

The minimum information shown on a network diagram is the task and the dependency – we would normally add other details, such as start and end dates – and these will be represented as boxes connected with lines.

Except in the case of trivial proiects, most people would not
these days consider the manual production of a PERT chart,
preferring to use automated planning packages.

Automated planning tools will carry out much of the
laborious number-crunching involved in this process,
leaving you time to properly analyse the results.

Slack (float)
Slack is the amount of time which a task can be delayed
without affecting any other tasks or the end date of the
project. It occurs when one task is dependent on
predecessors which may finish at different times.

From the Project Manager's point of view the existence of
slack in a plan may be beneficial as it does allow a certain
amount of latitude for planning when tasks should be done.
Too much slack and you might find yourself with
undesirable peaks in resourcing.

The critical path
The critical path is established by tracing a line through
those tasks on the dependency network which have no slack
at all. This represents the path through the project where, if
any slippage is incurred, the final end date will also slip.

Most importantly, however, it shows the shortest possible
time in which the project can be achieved, and you can,
therefore, use it to determine when the project (or phase)
will be completed. Note, however, that to derive the genuine
critical path it must be calculated using the *elapsed* time
taken to complete a task, not the days effort.

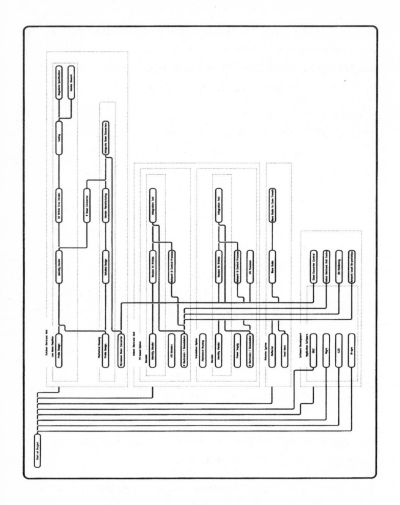

FIGURE 6 *Dependency diagram*

The critical path (and those tasks near the critical path, i.e. those with very little slack) represent those areas of the project upon which the Project Manager must concentrate his efforts to ensure that everything goes well.

Caution
The establishment of detailed dependency diagrams, even when using automated project management tools, can be a very complex and time-consuming process. In many projects the resultant network can be exceedingly complex. So complex, if fact, that it will do little to enhance your understanding of the project and have increasingly less use as a tool to monitor and control as the project progresses.

Dependencies, by their nature, tend to be between units of work at the bottom of the WBS. If it is possible to generalise the dependencies and so make links at a higher level in the WBS, then this will simplify the chart and allow it to be used as a communication tool both within and outside the project.

Responsibilities and resources

The Dependency Diagram at this point gives a strictly logical view of the project and in many ways represents what would happen in a perfect world.

Sadly, however, Project Managers operate in the real world of limited resources and fixed deadlines and the intrusion of these factors will change the view of the project. Where the network shows that a number of tasks can be executed in parallel, you may only have one person available to do them and they will, therefore, have to be done one after the other.

At this stage we are ready to assign individual project staff to particular tasks.

Each task should be made the responsibility of one and only one person; shared responsibility means that responsibility tends to get bucked. If possible, tasks should only be carried out by one person.

Clearly, this is not always possible as some tasks will genuinely need more than one person, or you may wish a task which could be done single-handedly to be done by several people in order to get it finished quickly. You should begin, however, by determining the optimum number of people to execute a task in the most efficient manner.

Calculating elapsed time to complete a task

- Determining optimum number of staff required to efficiently execute the task
- Determine the actual number of people available (and competent) to execute the task
- Determine their availability (expressed as a percentage) taking into account other duties, training commitments, holidays, sickness, etc.

$$\text{Elapsed time} = \frac{\text{Days effort * Staff availability}}{\text{Number of staff}}$$

You will also have to consider:

- the skill and experience levels of the staff assigned;
- their availability (it is normal to assume for estimating purposes that staff assigned full-time to a project are only productive four days a week at most to allow for sickness, administration, meetings, etc.);
- training, annual leave commitments and public holidays;
- 'unproductive' time spent in supervision; depending on the skill and experience of the staff being supervised, this could be as much as one day a week per person being supervised;
- the degree to which the optimum number of staff can be changed, some tasks simply cannot be completed any quicker no matter how much resource is applied.
- the constraints imposed by dependencies between tasks and externally imposed deadlines and milestones.

The Gantt Chart

The Gantt Chart is the primary tool which you will use for scheduling the project and then subsequently controlling it.

It is made up of a task information side (on the left) and a task bar side (on the right). The task information side holds such information as the name of the task, its WBS code, and who is responsible for it. The task bar is a line which graphically represents the period in time at which the task will be executed.

The precise content of a Gantt Chart should be determined by what you intend to use it for. As a communication tool to illustrate the project to senior management it would only be appropriate to include summary level tasks; if you are using it for your own purposes to monitor progress then more detail will be required.

A good planning tool will allow you to define the information you want displayed and the format in which it should appear.

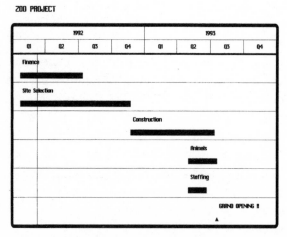

FIGURE 7 *Simple Gantt Chart*

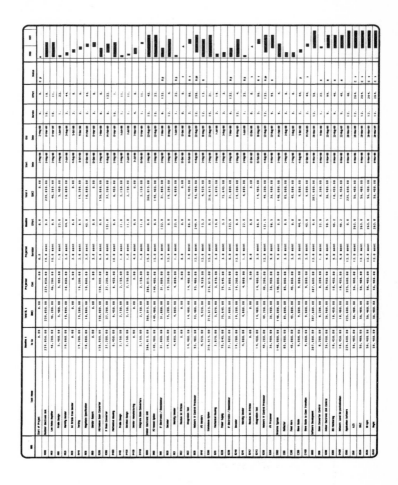

FIGURE 8 *Complex Gantt Chart*

The use of automated project management tools

HAVE A CHIP

PROJECT MANAGER

The development of automated project management tools over the years has transformed the way in which Project Managers can work. Because of their ability to manipulate large amounts of complex information they are capable of relieving the Project Manager of many hours of tedious work.

Not only can they store and manipulate large amounts of information, they allow you to make changes to your plans very quickly. Planning is an iterative process in which one is continually changing variables to arrive at the optimum plan. By using an automated tool we can experiment with 'what-if' scenarios to see, for instance, what the impact of applying more resource at a particular point on the plan might be in a matter of minutes. This might take hours or even days using pencil and paper.

An additional major benefit is in the production of reports. Detailed information on budgets and costs can be produced almost at the press of a button. Presentations to management can include high quality visual graphics.

If you are responsible for selecting the package which you will use do not forget to assess the quality of the output from the package. Some packages contain a high degree of sophistication in the processing they can perform, but let themselves down when it comes to producing reports that you can show anyone. As we discussed on Sunday, communication is a great part of the Project Manager's role.

Using sophisticated planning tools is, however, no substitute for sound project management and will not of itself guarantee the success of any project.

Quite the contrary; there is a great danger – particularly on large projects – that maintaining the plan can become the be all and end all of the project. The Project Manager's attention becomes diverted from managing the real problems and issues facing the project and spends more and more time ensuring that the plan, with its great complexities is perfect.

A plan is only that – a statement of intent – and it is putting it into practice which is at the heart of the Project Manager's job. We have spent a lot of time discussing planning because it is an important distinguishing part of the Project Manager's role. However, like all managers, most of his time is actually spent controlling the work.

Controlling projects – monitoring

Although planning and organising have been fairly intensive activities for the Project Manager, it is controlling the project which consumes the most time. He must exercise control over the process from the moment that he is appointed to the time that the project is finally completed.

Controlling projects is about ensuring that the project objectives are met; specifically those objectives of

- Time
- Cost
- Quality

We must ensure that the project is completed on the planned end-date, is completed within the specified budget and delivers what it promised to deliver to an acceptable quality. What these objectives are were described at the outset of the project in the Terms of Reference.

Today we will look at the area of control with specific reference to those three objectives. Control is made up of two parts: monitoring and then taking action. Today we will concentrate on the first aspect, monitoring.

Why do we control?

Managing change
The awkward thing about projects is that they never quite turn out as you expect them to. No matter how thorough

your planning, no matter how much senior management commitment you have solicited, no matter how well organised you have been ... things go wrong.

Factors which change projects

- The planning assumptions may have been wrong
  - there may be more to do than you anticipated
  - it might be harder than you anticipated
  - resources you depend on might not be available
- The requirements may change (very common)
- The deadline may change (usually earlier)
- The budget may be cut (try to complete projects within financial years)
- The priority of the project in the mind of senior mangement might change
- Barriers/resistance to change
- People make mistakes (usually large ones)
- Acts of God

All of these things – and many more – will conspire against your project and try to force it further and further away from achieving its objectives.

Naturally, you do not know what will go wrong at the outset of the project, although you will have allowed yourself a certain amount of contingency in terms of time and budget, simply because you know that *something* will go wrong.

By maintaining a high degree of control on the project – and this must extend beyond the immediate project team – you will be able to spot these potential dangers early enough to be able to do something about them.

Controlling projects is about identifying problems, working out what needs to be done to ameliorate them, and then doing it.

It is important that control is seen by the project team in this positive light. There is always a tendency to view control as merely an enormous chore for all those involved, whose only purpose is to give the Project Manager an opportunity to blame the guilty.

It should be portrayed as a process which is actually designed to help project staff in the work they do; to provide a mechanism by which they can flag problems they are suffering with, and through which solutions can be sought and implemented.

Pre-requisites for effective control

We will have already achieved a large part of the

prerequisites for control by the time we have invested in establishing the project. By progressing from the project objectives through to a detailed plan, we have broken the project up into controllable units.

Establishing a baseline
Deviations from the plan can only be measured and interpreted if we have a fixed view of what the original plan was. Fixing the original plan is known as 'setting the baseline'.

Establishing a formal control procedure
Control of projects should by and large be formalised. This is not to mean that it necessarily has to become a bureaucratic burden on all those involved. Merely that a regular and disciplined approach is taken to the control process.

As we mentioned above, project staff should understand the need for project control and they should also have a clear understanding of the process which is actually being used, and what in particular is being controlled.

What do we control?

As we said earlier, we will wish to control time, cost and quality. But what does that mean specifically?

Time
During the planning phase we will have established dates for major milestones on the project. These will have been widely publicised as part of raising the profile of the project. We have, therefore, a great interest in ensuring that these are adhered to.

We also defined start and end dates for all the activities which contribute to the attaining of these milestones. These also should be adhered to.

However, it is of little use to us if we get to our first major milestone date and discover that we have not made it. By recording basic data about the progress of tasks we can derive considerable amounts of information to assist us in its interpretation.

Time related progress data

- Status (future, started or complete)
- Elapsed time spent
- Days effort spent
- Estimate of days effort to go
- Estimate of elapsed time to go

Most automated planning tools can compare this information against your original plan (the baseline) and derive the following statistics relating to time:

- Proportional percent achieved
- Duration (projected)
- Duration variance
- Duration as % of baseline
- Effort variance
- End date (projected)
- End date variance
- Spent duration as % of baseline
- Spent effort percent
- To go duration
- To go effort
- To go duration as % of baseline

Here we are in severe danger of suffering from information overload, and you must choose carefully what is the minimum information you need to be able to answer the following questions:

- Have I made the progress I planned?
- Will I finish when I thought I would?

When determining progress it is important to remember that if you have spent half the time that you planned on a task it does not necessarily mean that you are halfway through it!

The most useful piece of information you can acquire about a task is how much longer (in terms of both effort and elapsed time) it will take to complete. By comparing this against your outstanding planned time to complete you can easily see if the task has slipped.

Cost

Control over costs is an area which is often neglected by Project Managers, particularly on projects whose only costs are staff costs and these are to a certain extent outside of the control of the project (e.g. where salaries are decided at a corporate level).

However, by monitoring costs the Project Manager will glean vital information about progress and the *value* of the work done. Costs can be used as a measure of progress.

From our planning exercises we will have determined resourcing profiles and therefore have a clear picture of how much the project will cost in staff terms overall, and what the profile of costs over time is. Other costs, such as for the acquisition of equipment, are usually fairly fixed. Do be aware, though, of costs which may be incurred in respect of services, consultancy, or cross-charges from other departments.

Remember, senior management tend to be particularly sensitive to costs, especially when things go wrong.

The degree of sophistication applied to the control of costs varies according to the type and size of project; it can be simple measurement of the number of people working on it, to complex accounting and control systems.

Some planning tools will go a long way to deriving statistics, but you should always remember that the quality of what you get out is directly proportional to the quality of what you put in.

The most important statistics are:

Estimated at Completion (EAC)
What the total cost of the project will be, as calculated by looking at the plan as it stands, i.e. costs incurred to date + scheduled costs
Budgeted at Completion (BAC)
The total cost derived from the plan before any work began
Actual Cost of Work Performed
The amount of money spent so far

Quality
Unlike time and cost, where we have units of measure such as days and pounds, the yardstick by which we measure quality is not so easy to find. Because it is difficult, it is often neglected.

The setting of quality standards involves having a clear specification of what the end product of the task should be, including whatever quality factors may be appropriate.

Views of quality are as varied as projects, but include such considerations as reliability, durability, accuracy, clarity and functionality.

Where quality factors are defined, then these should be measurable in some way. This might be the frequency of failures, the life-span, the number of corrections that have to be made to a document, or the number of comments made on a proposal.

Caution should be applied however, as statistics such as these can become distorted for perfectly sound reasons which are not necessarily a reflection on the quality.

Quality control is an important aspect – particularly in manufacturing processes – but a pre-requisite for it is quality assurance; establishing the right environment for quality to flourish.

Quality should be injected into the process from the outset. A common way of doing this is to develop a Quality Plan, which expresses your objectives for quality and how you will set about ensuring it.

This then becomes a key project document which is maintained to show when and how quality targets have been achieved, and any deviations from the Quality Plan.

The Quality Plan

- Define working methods and procedures
- Define standards for deliverables
- Define standards for supervision and review
- Define project checkpoints
- Define user involvement

A commitment to quality from the project team is vital to achieving it. It should be inculcated amongst the staff as being an essential, not a luxury, and ingrained in the culture of the project.

Progress reporting

Monitoring of time, cost and quality requires the Project Manager to have detailed knowledge of the status of all the tasks currently being executed. There are a number of ways in which this information can be gathered:

Progress reporting

- Progress reports
- One-to-one progress meetings
- Group/project progress meetings
- Wandering about

You should use **all four** of these techniques, as each will enable you to discover different pieces of information, or different perspectives on the same information.

Progress reports

The production of progress reports should be carried out on a strictly regular basis (usually weekly) by all those who are responsible for any planned activity. If this means that every single member of staff reports progress then so be it. The Project Manager does not necessarily have to read them all; they can be summarised by team leaders, junior managers and so on, to give overall progress reports for activities higher up the hierarchy on the WBS.

We have already mentioned that the whole area of control should be portrayed as genuinely being in the interests of the project staff.

Progress reports should, therefore, be as easy to complete as possible (which also helps you having to read them). A standardised form which shows the work done in a period, deviations from the plan, work for the next period, and any know problems, is ideal. An example is shown overleaf.

PROGRESS REPORT

Author	Mark Brown		Report Number	26	
Dept	Publishing		Week Commencing	22-7-92	

WBS Code	Task Name	Time Spent This Period	Estimate to Complete	Progress (Note 1)	Estimated Completion Date	Status (Note 2)
1.7.6	Receive "Report Writing in a Week"	0	0	0	22-7-92	Complete
1.7.7	Review "Report Writing" manuscript	3	4	-2	31-7-92	Started
7.1.9	Prepare monthly report for Board	1	0	+1	26-7-92	Complete
4.3.2	Paris Conference	1	0	0	25-7-92	Complete

Highlights this Period

1. Manuscript for "Successful Report Writing in a Week" delivered on time.

2. Monthly report to Board completed.

3. Paris conference a great success !

Problems Encountered this Period

Nature of Problem	Impact	Suggested Action
Report Writing" MS has been hand-written in green crayon and the author has adopted a prose style reminiscent of Marcel Proust.	1.7.7 will take an extra 2 days.	1. Send author on report writing course. 2. Warn graphics of delay.

Activities Planned for Next Period

1. Complete review of "Report Writing".

2. Presentation to Board.

3. Staff appraisals.

Note 1: Progress = Time Spent to Date + Estimate to Complete - Original Estimate
Note 2: Future/Started/Complete

Signed	
Date	

FIGURE 9 *Progress Report*

You will notice that the report calls for the writer to make comparison with the Project Plan and to reconsider the estimates to complete the work.

Although you may often see it, asking people to give a 'percentage complete' figure is usually less than satisfactory as it is only too easy to give a figure which reflects the percentage of planned time spent. By forcing staff to actively reconsider how much more time is really needed you will get a much more accurate picture of the genuine progress.

Progress reporting is not, however, all one way. The Project Manager himself will be expected to report to a number of other people/bodies, including the Sponsor.

Like all reports, the frequency, style, amount of detail and actual content will be varied to suit the particular audience.

Remembering that one of the key roles of the Project Manager as a communicator is to maintain commitment to the project, it is often a good idea to give some of these reports (especially those to senior management) in the form of presentations.

One-to-one progress meetings
Meetings with individual members of the project team, although time-consuming, are probably the best means of assessing progress.

It is important, however, that these meetings are well-structured and reasonably formalised. The purpose of the meeting is to assess progress and discuss any problems; it is not to have a generalised chat about how things are going – save that for by the coffee machine !

The best vehicle for structuring the meeting is the progress report. Each activity on it should be discussed – even if there are no problems associated with it.

Particular problems which have been identified on the progress report should be discussed in more detail in order to gain a real understanding of why the problem has occurred and what can be done about it.

Adopting the right style for the meetings is crucial to their effectiveness. There should be no atmosphere of blame or recrimination. Staff should be encouraged to approach the meetings with an honest and open attitude and not in fear that they are to be hauled over the coals. Praise should be lavished generously when things have gone well.

One-to-one meetings are also the best opportunity for the Project Manager to inspect quality himself. A golden rule of project monitoring is 'Everyone will lie to you!'. This may sound a little harsh on your trusted team, but I would suggest that it is not a bad position from which to start.

It is very easy for tasks to be only 95% complete when you are told that they are finished, so ask to see the finished report, the user's sign-off, the testing certificate, or whatever. There is no substitute for seeing it yourself.

Group/project progress meetings
Meetings of the entire project team (or groups within it if the project is too large to bring it all together regularly) are useful, but need to be carefully managed.

Their primary purpose is to ensure that all parts of the project are aware of what other parts are doing, and any issues that have arisen.

Whilst it is important that team spirit is fostered, you should always be aware that people will show greater reluctance to disclose problems in their own areas in a large group. If there are problems to be discussed at this level, then these should have been identified and corrective action agreed between the relevant parties and the Project Manager *before* the meeting.

Using technology

Many organisations now make extensive use of electronic mail and groupware. These are immensely valuable tools to Project Managers, both for the transmission of information to you, and for the dissemination of information (including the project library) around the project team. In the case of projects which have geographically dispersed teams, particularly if they are operating in different time zones, these tools should be considered indispensable.

Wandering about

Do it ! You will find out more about the project by doing this than any other way. By talking to your staff, especially the ones doing the actual work in an informal environment you will be able to grasp that intangible 'feel' of how well the project is going, and you will also be able to pick up on issues and problems as they arise, and before they have had time to embed themselves.

Controlling projects – taking action

Yesterday we discussed the ways in which the Project Manager can gather information which will tell him the status of work being undertaken on the project. Today we will look at what we must do with all that information; how to keep the project on course and see it to a successful conclusion.

Controlling projects

- Assessing the situation
- Impact analysis
- Resolving issues and problems
- Controlling change
- Completing the project

Control is the heart of what the Project Manager does – anyone can collate the information we discussed on Thursday, say 'what a shame' and file it, but it is up to the Project Manager to do something about it.

DON'T WORRY – I'M KEEPING A TIGHT HOLD

Assessing the situation

Prevention is, of course, better than cure, and this is why we have expended so much effort on producing a plan for time, cost and quality in which we have confidence. However, things will start happening differently from how you expected almost from the moment the project begins. Activities will start or complete late, costs will escalate and quality will fall.

You must be able to assess the impact of these occurrences on the overall project. To do this you must ask yourself a number of questions:

Assessing the situation

- How much will this effect other activities?
- What must I do to correct this particular problem?
- What must I do to put the project back on track?
- Why did it happen?
- What must I do to ensure that it does not happen again?

Most problems can be rectified provided that they are caught early enough. This is why we have emphasised the importance of regular and honest progress reporting.

Problems come in all sorts of shapes and sizes so it is hard to generalise about an approach to their resolution. A one-day slip on the plan may have no impact whatsoever if there is sufficient slack in the plan to cover it. On the other hand, there may be a one-day window in which something has to be done, and missing it might be disastrous.

Impact analysis

Establishing the impact of changes, whether brought about
internally or through something happening outside of the
project, cannot be done by the Project Manager single-
handedly.

In the same way that the flap of a butterfly's wing in Brazil
affects the climate in Europe, so the knock-on effect of change
anywhere in the project is likely to be felt everywhere else.
This rippling effect should not be underestimated, and –
within reason and depending on the sensitivity of the
circumstances – consultation should be as wide as possible.

You should note, however, that this will not only be people
with 'downstream' tasks; changes – particularly changes in
the specification of a product – could well have legal, health
and safety, marketing, personnel and other implications.

Once again, it is not just a question of gathering information; we have to analyse it to assess its implications.

If it is taking twice as long as planned to define the specification of a product, does that mean that it will take twice as long to build it and twice as long to test it? Is this a one-off, or are all our estimates to do with specification suspect? Do we have the right staff working on specification? Is the approach wrong?

All of these questions and more need to be answered, and can only be answered on the basis of your own experience and knowledge, supplemented by the expertise of those in individual areas.

Where you can look for a degree of help, though, is in the impact of problems and changes on the plans. If you are using automated planning tools, into which you have recorded the dependencies between tasks, you can very quickly feed in the revised effort estimates from the Impact Analysis, and so calculate revised end dates for all tasks and the project itself.

The dependency network diagram which we constructed as part of the planning process can be used to see which tasks are directly affected by one particular task slipping its planned completion date.

The planning tool will also give you a clear picture on costs and how your resourcing profile is affected.

If it is a major change, you may be forced into some substantial replanning.

Resolving issues and problems

Although action to resolve issues will be as varied as the different types of problem that will occur as a project, it can be generalised into several basic categories:

Resolving problems and issues

- Genuinely creative solutions to problems
- Using contingency
- Applying more resources
- Slipping the completion dates
- De-scoping
- Making sure it does not happen again

Note: there is no 'do nothing' option. Problems will not go away of their own accord, nor will they become more tolerable with time. They should be identified and resolved at the earliest possible opportunity.

Apart from the first and second approaches given above, resolving most problems implies a degree of compromise on your objectives of cost, time or quality.

Genuinely creative solutions

This is the ideal way to resolve a problem, but naturally the hardest. We can all lie awake at night seeking that flash of inspiration which will provide us with the answer to some acute problem; it rarely comes.

Re-examine the plan and particularly the planning assumptions. What may have appeared to be the only way to do something when you devised the plan might now be one of a number of ways, some of which may be better (and hopefully cheaper and faster).

Resource constraints may have forced you into doing things at certain times and in a particular order. Check if these resource constraints still exist as it might be possible to juggle some of the work.

On particularly long projects you may find that emergent technology or new techniques allow you to review your estimating assumptions.

Look again at the dependencies that are built in to the plan. Ask yourself if they really are finish-to-start dependencies, or if the second task can actually start with an incomplete input. (Apply caution here: it may impact quality and running tasks in parallel which are ideally done one after the other requires very careful management.)

Using contingency

You had the foresight to build contingency into the plans for this very eventuality, so use it! Be aware though that once it is all gone you cannot get it back again, and there might be times when your need of it will be greater. So use your contingency only when you really have no choice and monitor and control it carefully.

Applying more resources

Assigning more people to an activity which is running late is the most common means of rectifying a potential slippage. It is less desirable than whatever imaginative brainwaves we may have come up with earlier, but more so than the other two as it should not adversely affect your objectives of time and quality.

It will, of course, affect cost, but in the majority of projects time and quality tend to be considered more important.

Additional resource can be applied to tasks by moving staff off less important tasks (or at least tasks which are further away from the critical path). Be aware, though, that you may simply be deferring problems until later by doing this.

Alternatively, staff can be brought in from outside the project on a temporary basis, either from elsewhere in the organisation or by hiring contractors or consultants with specialist skills. Be aware, though, that this may be resented by the project staff who may see it as an unfavourable reflection on their own performance, and ensure that it is presented in a constructive and non-threatening manner.

Improvements in productivity tend to involve longer-term measures than you might be considering but you will always have the option of asking the staff to work additional hours, overtime and weekends. This must, however, be seen as a short-term solution of a recognisable crisis; in the long-term it will sap morale and probably reduce overall productivity.

Some further words of caution regarding applying additional resource:

Firstly, not all tasks can be completed more quickly simply by applying extra resource: two women cannot have a baby in four and a half months.

Secondly, bringing in staff from outside of the project may involve existing staff spending a lot of time teaching and supervising the newcomers. Do not underestimate either the amount of time it takes for people to get up to speed on the intricacies and issues of the project (no two projects are alike) and do not underestimate the impact it will have on other people's work.

Thirdly, beware of 'robbing Peter to pay Paul'. There is no point in moving staff onto a critical task if the first task is going to suffer as a result.

Slipping the completion dates
This is, of course, a highly undesirable course of action to have to take, although there may be times when you have no alternative.

This may mean that a particular task will be late, that a milestone will not be achieved on time, or even that the overall project will be delivered late.

Late achievement of published milestones or slippage of the overall project will usually require the authority of the project sponsor.

De-scoping
De-scoping means delivering less than you originally intended. It is a classic means of delivering something on time, and appropriate only if none of the above approaches will work and the project is in danger of being cancelled.

It is, of course, a serious compromising of the quality objective, but by delivering the minimum requirement on time, and leaving the 'nice-to-haves' until later (Phase 2 of the project), you at least preserve the organisation's investment in the work done to date.

Again, this should normally only be done with the consent of the project sponsor and in consultation with the users of the project's major deliverables.

Making sure it does not happen again

By and large the above approaches will involve taking tactical steps to resolve an immediate problem. It is equally important to ensure that the problem does not recur, either later on this project, or on other projects elsewhere in the organisation.

You should therefore examine – in a non-recriminatory manner – the root causes of the problem and what measures can be put in place to ameliorate them.

Areas worthy of review might be:

Causes of problems

- Estimating procedures
- Training policies
- Recruitment policies
- Quality control procedures
- Management control practices
- The culture of the organisation
- Staff motivational factors

Finding and implementing remedies to these sorts of problems is often outside of the immediate control of the Project Manager, but you should remember that as Project Manager you also have a duty to the organisation as a whole, and not just a single-minded devotion to your own project.

Furthermore, these may well be problems which are deeply embedded in the structure and culture of an organisation and will take a long period, possibly years, to change.

Controlling change

Ironically for the Project Manager, whose own role is to effect change elsewhere, change is his worst enemy. It destabilises all aspects of the project; the staff, the plan, the budget and the final product itself.

It was for this reason that we placed so much emphasis earlier in the week on clearly defining the scope of the project and ensuring that all project phases involved review and sign-off by the user.

But requirements will change during the course of a project, particularly longer ones. We cannot freeze the outside world during the course of a project and so we should not be too dogmatic about resisting change.

What we can do, however, is ensure that change is properly controlled. This operates at two levels: fundamental changes to the project itself and detailed changes to the project deliverables.

Project changes
Significant changes to the project will usually involve amending the original Terms of Reference, usually the scope, but sometimes the project objectives or the approach.

Requests for change, whether from outside or from within the project team, should be subject to both Impact Analysis and a degree of Cost-Benefit Analysis.

Departures from the original Terms of Reference can only be made with the authority or consent of those who originally agreed them; the project sponsor and the senior user management.

So that an informed decision on whether or not to accept the change can be made, the decision-makers must have a clear understanding of what is involved.

Remember that the further a project progresses, the more expensive change becomes and it is important to be able to distinguish between what is absolutely necessary and what would be nice to have.

At some point in the project you will have to 'freeze' the specification. This is never popular with users, but is the only way of ensuring that the project does not continue to grow and grow as more features are requested.

Project deliverables
Apart from the final end product which the project is to deliver, most of the project's deliverables will be paper – lots of it; specifications, designs, reports, analyses, and plans.

These should all be closely controlled and this is often a function of the Project Office. You should therefore establish document control procedures which:

Document control procedures

- Identify which documents are to be controlled
- Specify the prime author of each document
- Specify where the master copy is held
- List the names of copy recipients
- Detail procedures for raising changes
- Detail procedures for reviewing changes
- Specify version numbering conventions

Completing the project

Finally the happy day has come. The work is done, the product has been accepted, implemented and is being used by thousands of satisfied customers.

Or are they ?

A *project review* should be conducted some time after project completion with the following objectives:

Project review objectives

- To measure the success of the project
- To determine the need for further work
- To identify any lessons learnt

Personal qualities of the Project Manager

Throughout the week we have been looking at the project very much in terms of its mechanics; thinking about the project, its tasks and the resources which will be used.

In most projects the main resource is **people** and so today we will look at some of the personal qualities which a Project Manager must bring to bear.

Personal qualities of the Project Manager

- Motivating
- Delegating
- Communicating
- Leading

Successful management of people is a complex topic and by no means unique to project management. We must, however, recognise that project management is as much about handling people as anything else.

Unfortunately there are no prescriptive tools or techniques which can be applied to turn someone into a good people-manager.

Motivating

No matter how well planned and organised a project may be, its chances of success without the commitment of the project team are limited. It is largely up to the Project Manager to ensure that the project enjoys a culture and an atmosphere which is conducive to achieving the project objectives.

When you look for people to be on the team you will naturally look for people who are dynamic, committed, responsible, intelligent, forward-thinking, highly-skilled, and good team-players.

All admirable qualities, certainly, but qualities which require nurturing by the Project Manager. It may sound trite to say that a happy project team will result in a successful project – it won't. But we must nonetheless try to ensure that the project team actually *wants* to do the work and, moreover, wants to do it the way you want.

The key to motivating people is achieving a degree of alignment between their personal objectives and the project objectives. You must be able to show that people will actually get what they want by doing what you want.

Of course working out what individual people want is a tricky business and much has been written on the subject of motivation in general.

Motivation theories

- *Maslow* – A hierarchy of needs ranging from physical to existential
- *Herzberg* – Distinguishing between what motivates and what demotivates
- *Pope* – 'Deadly Sin Theory'; people are motivated by pride, lust, anger, gluttony, envy, sloth and covetousness

---

What these and other theories tell us is that different people are motivated by different things. No surprise perhaps, but it means that we must know and understand the individuals we are trying to motivate if we are to be able to work out what it is that drives them.

Pay and rations

Contrary to popular belief, pay is not a great motivator. Large pay rises may induce a short-term sense of well-being, but this quickly fades.

This is fortunate, as on many projects an individual's pay is not within the Project Manager's direct control. However, satisfactory pay is a pre-requisite for getting any work at all out of your staff, let alone high performance.

You should therefore ensure that the pay your project staff receive is competitive (to stop them from leaving) and fair (to prevent internal divisions). Pay is a quantifiable measure of how well the organisation thinks a member of staff is doing.

Bonuses for completing projects on time are, likewise, not terribly good motivators. They can be used, however, if you are suffering from debilitating turnover of staff and need to stabilise the situation at least for the duration of the project.

Non-financial incentives

Non-financial incentives are, however, within the direct control of the Project Manager. You should look for ways of meeting the following needs which people have:

> *Motivating factors*
>
> - Quality of work (interesting, challenging and useful)
> - Sense of belonging (to project team)
> - Feeling of involvement
> - Sense of achievement
> - Recognition of success and effort
> - Opportunity for development and progression
> - Fufilment of skills and abilities
> - Increased responsibility

Finding ways of fulfilling these needs varies from individual to individual, and it is clearly important that you get to know your staff well on a personal level.

Delegating

Not only does delegation, in the long run, make your own life easier, but it also enhances the working lives of your staff by making them feel involved in and responsible for the work being done.

Delegation is a delicate art and a balance must be drawn between complete abdication of your personal responsibilities and being dictatorial.

There is a natural reluctance in most people to delegate. This stems usually from a lack of trust or a belief that you could do the job better yourself. Even if this is the case it is no excuse not to delegate.

Some tasks should not be delegated (especially those involving personnel issues), but for many it is an efficient means of getting the work done and of developing the staff.

When delegating you should make clear what needs to be done and why, when it should be done by and how much authority you are giving the person.

Communicating

We discussed the need for the Project Manager to be a communicator when we described his role on Sunday. In a nutshell, we communicate in order to influence the behaviour of other people.

Differing circumstances dictate what is the appropriate style in which we should do this, and the Project Manager must be sensitive to both the nature of his message and its audience.

Above all he should be sufficiently flexible in his approach and pick the appropriate style in the broad range from ordering, through negotiating, persuading, advising and listening (for we must remember that effective communication is a two-way process).

Effective communication skills – in all circumstances – are vital to any Project Manager. Whereas the line manager can rely to a great extent on his position in the organisation to influence others, the Project Manager must fall back on his personality to do so.

Leadership

Leadership is one of the less easily taught aspects of management. To be effective, a manager must be able to lead, to inspire others to follow him. This need is all the stronger in project management because a project relies so much on the commitment and loyalty of those involved.

Unfortunately charisma cannot be bottled and applied in liberal doses every morning. However, a number of adjectives spring to mind when describing leaders.

Leadership qualities	
• Dynamic	• Confident
• Visionary	• Imaginative
• Flexible	• Analytic
• Creative	• Decisive
• Patient	• Sympathetic
• Persistent	• Organised
• Assertive	• Goal-driven
• Persuasive	• Charismatic

Each of these qualities will be called upon during a project; the successful leader will instinctively know the right approach to take in the right circumstance.

Choosing a Project Manager

Project management is not something which can be done by anyone, and all too often there is an assumption that if someone can manage a department then that same person can manage a project.

The role of the Project Manager is an important one and fundamental to the success of any project. Organisations make large investments in projects and should make similar investments in the people they call upon to manage those projects.

It calls for additional skills and characteristics over and above those which are normally required for line management.

These are skills which can mostly be learnt through training and, above all, experience. Many organisations have now instituted project management development programmes which reflect its position as a professional discipline in its own right.

Through this week we have concentrated on how the Project Manager ensures that other people deliver for the project within constraints of time, cost and quality. We should not forget, however, that the Project Manager's own deliverables are amongst the most important in the project.

Project Manager's deliverables

- Terms of Reference or project definition
- Milestone plan
- Budget
- Work Breakdown Structure
- Project Organisation chart
- Responsibility chart
- Task definitions
- Deliverable definitions
- Quality plan
- Dependency chart
- List of planning and estimating assumptions
- Gantt Chart
- Progress reporting standards
- Change control standards
- Progress reports
- End-of-phase reports
- Project review report